LIFE IN PONDS

LISA REGAN

WAYLAND

First published in Great Britain in 2019
by Wayland
Copyright © Hodder and Stoughton, 2019

Created for Wayland by www.squareandcircus.co.uk
Design and illustrations: Supriya Sahai
Editor: John Hort

HB ISBN: 978 1 5263 1105 4
PB ISBN: 978 1 5263 1106 1

Printed and bound in China

Wayland, an imprint of
Hachette Children's Group
Part of Hodder and Stoughton
Carmelite House
50 Victoria Embankment
London EC4Y 0DZ
An Hachette UK Company
www.hachette.co.uk
www.hachettechildrens.co.uk

Picture credits: iStock—Jason Ondreicka 14d; Shutterstock—Joe
Dunckley 4a; Alizada Studios 4b; Wollertz 5a; Aleksandar Todorovic
5b; Katvic 5c; Danita Delmont 7a; Eric Broder Van Dyke 7b;
Stephan Morris 8a; Tatiana53 8b; Konstantin Baidin 8c; L Rider
9a; Kevin McKeever 9b; Roberto Sorin 9c; MUUBEER 10a; Pavel
Krasensky 10b; Rattiya Thongdumhyu 10c; Eric Isselee 10d; ULD
photo life 10e; Troutnut 10f; Henri Koskinen 10g; khlungcenter 11a;
RachelKolokoffHopper 11b; Anton Kozyrev 11c; Martin Pelanek 11d;
optimarc 11e; Rostislav Stefanek 12a; 12b; 12d; 13a; 13d; FedBul 12c;
Vladimir Wrangel 13b; Krzysztof Odziomek 13c; Cosmin Manci
14a; Toby Rowland 14b; Tom Reichner 14c; Vitalii Hulai 15a; Hintau
Aliaksei 15b; Darkfoxelixir 16; Kim Howell 17a; Mira Anggun Sari 17b;
Nigel Dowsett 18a; Pim Leijen 18b, Christian Weber 18c; Allexxandar
18d; Michael Cummings 18e; Erwan LOISON 19a; Ferenc Cegledi 19b;
Collins93 19c; Emilio100 19d; Nikolay Zaborskikh 19e; Amy Lutz 21;
Anneka 21; Mark Bridger 22a; Puffin's Pictures 22b; Eric Isselee 22c;
Holly Kuchera 22d; Baisa 23a; Michael Schober 22b; Michiel de Wit
23c; Erni 23d; Dr.Pixel 23e; jo Crebbin 23f; Sang Low PS 24a; Kristi
Blokhin 24b; matthew25 24c; elitravo 24d; IvanaJankovic 24e; David
Louis Econopouly 25a; Larina Marina 25b; Koldunov 25c; Eileen
Kumpf 25d; Christelle Bosch 26; DMS Foto 27; Melissa King 28;
Alexmalexra 29. Cover: Yuriy Kulik.

BE CAREFUL

Do not go near water
without adult supervision.

CONTENTS

WHAT ARE LAKES AND PONDS?

A lake is a large area of water surrounded by land. Lakes are found all around the world, and come in a variety of sizes and shapes. Whatever their size, they are important **ecosystems** and are home to a large number of plants and animals.

DID YOU KNOW?

Some lakes and ponds are man-made. Lots of people build a pond in their garden to attract wildlife. A lake that is built to store water for human use is called a **reservoir**.

Lakes like Ullswater (pictured) in the English Lake District were formed by glaciers.

Lake or pond?

A pond is small area of still, fresh water. Ponds are usually smaller and shallower than lakes. Sunlight can reach all the way to the bottom, allowing plants to grow. A lake may only have plants around its edge, as the water is too deep to allow sunlight to pass through. As a result, a lake will be warmer at the top and become cooler as the water gets deeper.

Walden Pond in Massachusetts, USA, is actually a lake, as it's too big and deep to be a real pond.

Oregon's Crater Lake is the deepest volcanic lake in the US.

Making a lake

A lake sits in a hollow in the ground. There are different ways in which the hollow can be formed. The crater of an inactive volcano can fill with rain or melted snow to make a **volcanic lake**. Rivers change course over time and as they do, parts may be cut off to leave **oxbow lakes**. Movement in the Earth's crust can also form lakes. The crust is divided into sections called tectonic plates, so the lakes are known as **tectonic lakes**. Many of the world's largest and most famous lakes, including the Great Lakes in North America, were formed a long time ago by glaciers scraping across the land. They carved large pits or left rocky dams that trapped water and created **glacial lakes**.

This winding river will eventually form a new oxbow lake.

Lake Baikal is the world's oldest lake, and is about 25 million years old.

Around the world

The deepest lake in the world is Lake Baikal in Russia. It is a tectonic lake, formed where two sections of the Earth's crust are slowly pulling apart. Lake Baikal contains more water than all five of North America's Great Lakes added together, and holds 20 per cent of the world's fresh water. It has an area of 31,722 km and a depth of 1,642 m.

THE WATER CYCLE

All the water on Earth is constantly on the move in the water cycle. The same water goes around and around, **evaporating** from lakes and ponds, as well as seas and oceans, to become clouds. It then falls back to Earth.

The water cycle

Condensation

Transpiration

Evaporation

Precipitation

Water also enters the water cycle from people, through perspiration (sweat), and plants, through **transpiration.**

Around and around

Heat from the Sun warms up oceans, lakes, rivers and puddles. This makes the water evaporate: it turns into a gas called water vapour. The water vapour rises into the sky and begins to cool again, making it **condense** and turn back into water droplets. These form clouds and eventually become too heavy to stay in the sky. They fall back to Earth as **precipitation** (rain, snow, hail or sleet).

Part-time ponds

Seasonal ponds may appear during rainy periods, stay until summer and then dry up again. They often look like a huge puddle in the woods or a field. Fish cannot live in them, which makes them an important breeding ground for other creatures. Insects and amphibians lay their eggs in the water, knowing they will hatch without being eaten.

Open or closed?

Lakes can contain either fresh water or salt water. If the water can leave the lake via a river, the lake is open. If there are no outlets, the lake is closed. The only way water escapes from a closed lake is by evaporation. Any minerals that were dissolved in the water are left behind, and this eventually makes the water turn salty.

All freshwater lakes are open, including Lake Como in Italy.

Salt lakes

Some lakes are so salty that they are known as seas. However, they are still lakes as they are enclosed bodies of water. The largest of them all is the Caspian Sea on the border of Europe and Asia. The Caspian Sea is salty, but not as salty as the oceans. The Dead Sea is also a lake in western Asia, and is about ten times saltier than seawater!

TRY THIS...

WATCH THE WATER CYCLE

You can create your own miniature water cycle at home.

- Ask an adult to help you half-fill a clean glass jar with hot water.

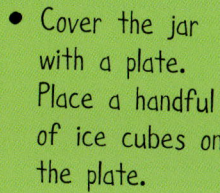

- Cover the jar with a plate. Place a handful of ice cubes on the plate.

- Wait and watch as 'rain' forms on the underside of the plate and drips back down into the water.

The salt from Utah's Great Salt Lake can be harvested and sold.

LIFE IN THE WATER

A pond or lake often contains every major group of living things, from tiny bacteria to insects, fish and amphibians. Reptiles, mammals and birds live in or near lakes and ponds, and eat water creatures and plants. In dry areas, a lake may act as a watering hole where land animals gather to drink.

Some insects can run across the top of the water.

Water birds such as the moorhen often make their nest in plants at the water's edge.

Irises and rushes grow at the edge with their roots in wet soil.

Algae forms a green coating on the surface. They aren't plants but do photosynthesise.

Large mammals visit to drink at the water's edge.

Growing in the water

Aquatic plants, such as water lilies (pictured), have spongy leaves and stems to help them survive in the water. Like all plants, they make their own food through a process called **photosynthesis**. Using the energy in sunlight, they convert carbon dioxide and water into sugar, which helps them grow. They release oxygen as a by-product.

Some water beetles carry a bubble of air so they can breathe underwater.

TRY THIS...

MAKE OXYGEN BUBBLES

Watch pond plants photosynthesise and produce oxygen before your very eyes!

- Fill a large bowl with clean water. Add a few sprigs of Canadian pondweed.
- Place the bowl in the sunshine, or next to a bright light.
- After a while, you should start to see bubbles forming in the water. These are the oxygen bubbles being made by the plant.

Frogs lay their eggs in the water.

FRESHWATER MINIBEASTS

A healthy lake or pond will have dragonflies and damselflies darting around. Leeches, midge **larvae** and horse flies are a sign of a less healthy pond, possibly with **stagnant** water and low oxygen levels.

Dragonfly

A dragonfly has strong transparent wings that allow it to dip and dive like a fighter plane. Their young are called **nymphs** and feed on aquatic animals.

Caddisfly

Closely related to moths and butterflies, these insects have two pairs of delicate but hairy wings. Their aquatic larvae build a case from silk and gravel for protection.

Water spider

Known as the diving bell spider, this is the only type of spider that can sleep, eat, mate and reproduce underwater. It is found in ponds and lakes in Europe and Asia.

Leech

These soft carnivorous creatures are closely related to earthworms. They live in the water and attach themselves to their prey so they can suck its blood.

Snail

Some freshwater snails can live underwater as they have gills for breathing. Others have to get to the surface to breathe air.

DID YOU KNOW?

Hydra are a type of tiny creature found in lakes and ponds. They have a long tube-shaped body and a mouth surrounded by tentacles. They can rebuild damaged body parts, so they don't grow old or die of old age.

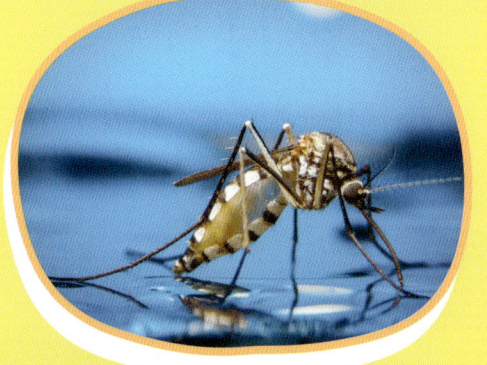

Midge

Look out for swarms of these tiny two-winged flies, sometimes called gnats, that look a little like mosquitoes. Some of them bite, and most of them lay their eggs in the water.

Mosquito

Female mosquitoes lay their eggs in ponds so that their young can feed on tiny creatures in the water when they hatch.

Water boatman

You may have to use a net to find these beetles, as they swim at the bottom of a pond, feeding on plants and algae.

TRY THIS...

WALKING ON WATER

Find out how some insects stay on top of the water without sinking.

- Drop a paperclip into a cup of water. Does it sink or float?

- Now gently place the paperclip flat on the surface. Can you get it to float?

- If it sinks, try resting it on a small piece of kitchen paper. When the paper sinks, the paperclip should stay afloat.

- Water molecules at the surface are attracted to each other and 'stick' together, acting as if there is a skin on the top of the water. This is known as surface tension. It is what allows the paperclip and some water insects to stay afloat.

Diving beetle

These predators feed on tadpoles and other small creatures, biting them with sharp mouthparts. The larvae are so fierce they are nicknamed water tigers.

Pond skater

Also known as water striders, these insects have long, thin legs covered with tiny hairs. These hairs allow them to walk across the water's surface using surface tension.

FRESHWATER FISH

Many garden ponds have decorative fish in them, such as goldfish or koi carp. In nature, ponds and lakes have a much wider variety of fish, of all shapes and sizes.

Minnow

Minnows are tiny, generally growing to a maximum of 10 cm long. They live together in groups called shoals and are eaten by many birds, aquatic mammals and larger fish.

Wels catfish

Native to central and eastern Europe, these slimy, scaleless fish have been introduced all over Europe and across Asia for recreational fishing. They have long barbels by their mouth, and are the biggest freshwater fish.

DID YOU KNOW?

Catfish can live to be over fifty years old!

Perch

A small, striped fish, the perch has a row of sharp spines along its dorsal (back) fin. Their stripes camouflage them, keeping them safe from predatory birds.

Carp

This bronze-coloured fish can grow very big and has a large, rounded body and powerful fins. It pokes around at the bottom of a lake looking for insects, snails and worms to eat.

Rudd

Look out for this fish in summer, when it breaks the surface of the water to eat small insects.

Stickleback

Small but distinctive, the most common type of stickleback has three spines on its back. In spring the male's underside turns red to show it is ready to mate.

Tench

Tench are found across Europe and Asia. Their scales are much smaller than most other fish, making them look smooth. They live in lakes with lots of vegetation, and mostly feed at night.

Pike

A fierce predator, the pike's large mouth is filled with razor-sharp, backward pointing teeth. It has a long thin body for making fast movements in the water.

TRY THIS...

MAKE A WATER-SCOPE

Use this to help you see what is under the water much more clearly.

- You will need a large empty drink carton, such as a tetrapak with a pouring spout.

- Ask an adult to cut off the bottom of the carton. Ask them to also cut a section off the top, leaving a viewing hole around the size of your palm.

- Cover the bottom with cling film, using rubber bands to hold it in place. Stretch it as tight and as smooth as possible.

- Tape around the top of the cling film with duct tape.

- Hold the sealed end of your water-scope underwater and look through the top. Keep it still so you don't frighten off any creatures.

REMEMBER!

Do not go near the water without adult supervision.

13

AMPHIBIANS

Amphibians are animals that start life in the water and then live on land. They stay near the water as adults so they can lay their eggs there. Frogs, toads, newts and salamanders are all amphibians.

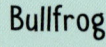

Spotted salamander

Spotted salamanders live in damp areas of forests in parts of North America. They stay close to ponds, where they lay their eggs in fresh water. They must keep their skin damp or they cannot breathe.

Common newt

A newt is a type of salamander. Newts shelter under stones during the day and search for insects to eat when it is cooler. Males grow a jagged crest on their back during mating season.

Eastern American toad

The warts of this toad contain a mildly poisonous liquid that helps prevent it being eaten by other animals.

Bullfrog

The American bullfrog is the largest North American frog and has a loud call. It has a varied diet, from small birds and reptiles to shellfish and snails.

What's the difference?

Frogs and toads can look similar – so which is which?

Moves in leaps and bounds

Smooth, moist skin

Slim body

Pointed nose

Crawls rather than hops

Rounded face and body

Thick, rough, warty skin

Short back legs

Long back legs

Webbed feet

Stays close to water

Separate toes

Can live in drier places

Common frog

Mostly **nocturnal**, this European frog can lighten or darken its skin to match its surroundings. It **hibernates** in the winter, finding shelter under leaves, stones or logs, or burrowing into pond mud.

Common toad

Found across Europe, this nocturnal toad hides in the daylight and appears as night falls. It feeds on slugs, worms and ants.

Frogs lay their eggs in a bundle called frogspawn.

Toads lay their eggs in long chains.

LIFE CYCLES

Mammal babies often look like miniature versions of their parents. This isn't the case for other animals, including amphibians and insects. They go through **metamorphosis**, changing their appearance as they grow.

DID YOU KNOW?

Aquatic insects often spend years in their nymph or larval stage before they become adults and leave the pond. Dragonfly nymphs usually live underwater for up to two years, although the golden-ringed dragonfly spends more than five years as a nymph.

Tadpoles eat their way out of the clear jelly that forms their eggs.

From spawn to adults

Amphibians begin life as eggs (called spawn) and hatch into tadpoles. Tadpoles breathe underwater with gills, like fish do. Gradually, the tadpoles lose their gills and their lungs develop so they can breathe out of the water. Nearly all amphibians lose their tail and grow legs so they can move around on dry land.

Life cycle of a frog

Frogspawn

Tadpole

A frog tadpole grows its back legs before its front legs.

Adult frog

Froglet (young frog)

Complete or incomplete?

There are two different life cycles for insects. Some go through complete metamorphosis. They hatch from an egg as a larva and then grow, shedding their outer layer (**moulting**) as they get bigger. The fully-grown larva then makes a **pupa** for itself, and when it emerges it is an adult with wings.

Butterflies, beetles and caddisflies undergo complete metamorphosis.

Complete metamorphosis

Eggs

Caterpillar

Pupa

Emerging adult

Incomplete metamorphosis

This adult dragonfly is emerging from its moulted skin.

Other insects go through incomplete metamorphosis. Their eggs hatch into nymphs, which often live in the water. The nymph grows and moults, growing wings inside its skin as it turns into an adult.

Dragonflies, damselflies and mayflies undergo incomplete metamorphosis.

17

WATER BIRDS

You will see many types of bird living in the trees around a pond or lake. Certain birds have adapted to live on the water where they fish or dive for food. They make their nests in nearby plants or even in the middle of lakes or ponds.

Ducks, geese and swans are all part of the same family of birds, often called waterfowl.

Great crested grebe

Loon
Found mainly in North America, these birds swallow small stones which help to grind down hard parts of their food, such as bones and shells.

Grebe
Grebes are brilliant at swimming but find it difficult to walk on dry land. Watch them dive for fish and reappear at the surface in a completely different place.

Coot
Coots have black feathers and a distinctive white shield above the beak. They run across the water during takeoff.

Heron
Their long beak is designed for catching fish, but these birds also eat small mammals, frogs and baby birds. There are several types, including the grey heron shown here.

Canada goose

Much larger than a duck, a goose has a longer neck and bigger, stronger wings. Canada geese are a common sight in North America and Europe.

Egret

Part of the heron family, egrets always have white or pale feathers. Like all herons, they have a long flexible neck.

Common Kingfisher

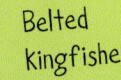

Belted Kingfisher

Kingfisher

Easily identified by their bright feathers, these birds can nevertheless be hard to find. They flit across the surface of the water looking for fish.

Swan

One of the largest flying birds, swans are usually white with a black or orange beak. Their babies are called cygnets and have grey fluffy feathers.

Duck

There are many species of duck and they have a variety of colours and patterns. Generally, they all have a short neck, round head and webbed feet to help them swim.

Adapted beaks

The shape of a bird's beak can give you a clue how it eats. The large sharp bill of a heron is used for stabbing its food while standing at the water's edge. Flat beaks are used for dabbling: a duck or swan will dip its head in the water to grab plants and bugs. Fishing birds have a pointed beak, with rough edges to hold onto their slippery prey. Some fly and then dive into the water, while others swim before they dive.

MORE ABOUT DUCKS

Ducks are closely related to swans and geese. They are found on every continent apart from Antarctica. There are many types, from dabbling ducks to diving ducks. There are even ducks with feet designed for perching in trees!

Feeding time

Some ducks have a specialist diet and mostly eat fish. Most types of duck, however, eat just about anything they can get in their beak. Their diet includes fish, crustaceans, insects, seeds, nuts and fruit, and they also nibble at grass and aquatic plants.

In the water

Ducks have short legs, a rounded body and a distinctive waddle when they walk. However, they are designed to move easily through the water. The webbing in between their toes acts like a paddle to push the maximum amount of water behind them, moving the duck forwards as it does so.

Male mallard duck

Females usually make more noise than males. Not all ducks quack; they also grunt, groan, growl, whistle and squeak.

Feathered friends

The top layer of a duck's feathers are covered with a waxy waterproof coating. A duck has to preen itself to look after these feathers. It rubs its beak near its tail to pick up a special oil that it then spreads over its body. Underneath the top feathers is a soft, fluffy layer called down that keeps the duck warm.

Female mallard duck

A female duck is called a <u>hen</u>, and a male is called a <u>drake</u>. The males usually have more brightly coloured feathers to help them attract a mate, while the hen is often brown for camouflage.

The top feathers are so watertight that a duck can dive under the water and its down feathers will not get wet.

Baby birds

Each spring, adult ducks make a nest and breed. The mother lays several eggs in the nest. Around four to five weeks later, the eggs hatch. The newborn ducklings cannot go in the water for the first couple of days as their small, fluffy feathers are not yet fully waterproof.

DID YOU KNOW?

After mating, male ducks lose lots of their feathers. They are unable to fly, and often take shelter out on the water to stay safe from predators.

MAMMALS AND REPTILES

Many mammals and reptiles are not suited to life in a lake or pond, but make their home on banks or shores. Some are good swimmers, and spend time in the water looking for food.

Water vole

Related to mice, water voles are short, stout mammals with sleek fur. North American water voles are larger than European water voles. They all make burrows in the banks of ponds, lakes and rivers, with an entrance into the water.

Mink

In the wild, mink live near the water to prey on frogs, fish, aquatic birds and small mammals. They are good swimmers and often dive to explore underwater holes and rocks.

Muskrat

Muskrats are medium-sized rodents, with a slightly flattened tail to help them swim. Muskrats feed on aquatic plants. They can close their ears to keep out water.

Otter

These super swimmers chase and catch fish, and can spend up to five hours each day hunting. Their sensitive whiskers feel tiny movements in the water, which help them to hunt.

Beaver

A beaver may burrow into the side of a lake, or gnaw down trees to dam a stream and make their own pond. They build their home, called a lodge, in the middle of a lake, pond or river.

Painted turtle

Turtles

Found across North America, the painted turtle feeds in the water but can often be seen sunbathing on logs or rocks. Stay away from the snapping turtle as it has sharp, powerful, beak-like jaws.

Snapping turtle

Smaller fore limb

Water shrew

This little creature feeds on small fish and insect larvae found at the bottom of a pond. The fur of a water shrew traps air bubbles, which make it float to the surface if it stops paddling during a dive.

TRY THIS...

Larger hind limb

ANIMAL TRACKING

Learn to read the signs left behind by your aquatic friends.

- Walk slowly around the pond, looking to each side of you. Pay particular attention to the tall plants. Can you see any nests among the stems?

- Can you see footprints? Can you identify what animal made them?

- Keep a record in a notebook. Draw the prints, or take a photo on a phone. Add the date, time and weather conditions.

- Always wash your hands properly after a nature walk.

Grass snake

Snakes

Some snakes swim in ponds and lakes, hunting for food. In Europe and Asia, the grass snake feeds mostly on amphibians. In the USA, look out for the cottonmouth, which is venomous and eats anything small enough to fit in its mouth.

Cottonmouth

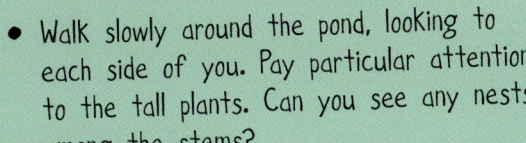

GROWING BY THE WATER

Plants growing in and around lakes and ponds provide food and shelter from predators. Some plants grow in the muddy bottom of the water, or float on top with their roots dangling down. Many plants have adapted to grow in the soggy ground at the water's edge. Their stalks are stronger than those of underwater plants.

Duckweed

Duckweed has lots of tiny round leaves that float on the surface to form a green carpet. It is a popular food, not only for ducks, but also for snails.

Milfoil

This plant has fine, feathery leaves that spread out in the water around the stem. Its tiny flowers poke above water level. It multiplies quickly and can take over a pond or lake, pushing out other plants.

Cattail

Also called reedmace or bulrushes, these distinctive plants grow sausage-shaped spikes on top of long stems. They flower and turn to fine fluff made of thousands of seeds that blow away on the wind.

Iris

This beautiful flower is easy to spot, with its three drooping petals around three smaller, upright petals. Its shape allows insects to land and gather nectar, and then transfer pollen to another iris.

Water lily

The leaves of a water lily are tough and leathery. They provide shade and shelter for creatures below. Their flowers appear in late spring or summer.

Annoying algae

Algae appear as green scum on the water's surface, or green slime coating rocks and the bottom of a pond or lake. Algae grow faster (known as algal bloom) if pollutants are added to the water, for example if detergents, fertiliser or sewage washes into the lake. Algae can harm other living things by using up **nutrients** needed by plants and reducing the amount of oxygen for insects and fish to breathe.

Fly

Common/soft rush

These clumps of tall stems provide food for moths and other insects, and are a good place for water birds to make their lakeside nests.

Sundew

These extraordinary plants have sticky tentacles to trap insects that are attracted by the plants' sweet smell. Sundews get very few minerals from the marshy soil they grow in, so they digest insects to get extra nutrients. The leaves have shiny drop-like edges, giving the plants their name.

TRY THIS...

Spearwort

Related to the buttercup, spearwort grows in the shallows. It is popular with bees and butterflies when its flowers appear in the summer.

MAKE A REED DIFFUSER

Your home will smell gorgeous!

- Ask an adult to cut four lengths of reed stem, about 30 cm long.

- Place the stems somewhere warm for a few days to dry out.

- Find a clean glass bottle with a narrow neck. Pour 3 cm of baby oil into the bottle. Add a few drops of essential oil and swirl them around.

- Place the dried reeds into the oil. It will gradually travel up the reeds and give off a scent. Flip the sticks over every other day, to keep the scent fresh.

A POND FOOD WEB

A pond or lake works as a freshwater ecosystem. The plants and animals link to each other as part of a food chain. These food chains join together to make a food web. It shows us what is eaten by what, from tiny **organisms** up to large predators.

Crayfish

Minnow

Dragonfly

Algae

Water weed

Mayfly (larva)

From bottom to top

Organisms that make their own food are at the bottom of a food chain. These can be plants or algae, and they are called **producers**. These are eaten by insects, fish and birds – primary **consumers**. The primary consumers might then become food for secondary consumers, such as snakes, bigger fish or fish-eating birds.

Swans eat mostly plant matter, including algae.

At the top

Consumers at the top of the food chain are called <u>apex predators</u>, such as this bald eagle. It is found near many lakes across North America, where it feeds on fish.

Kingfisher

Frog

Snake

TRY THIS...

GO POND-DIPPING

Make your own net and then inspect what you catch.

REMEMBER!
Do not go near the water without adult supervision.

- Cut the legs off an old pair of tights. Leave just enough fabric to tie tightly in a knot to form a net.

- Make a small slit in the waistband of the tights. This should allow you to feed a piece of stiff wire (a coat hanger is ideal) through the gap.

- Twist the two ends of wire together and push them into the hole at the end of a piece of garden cane.

- Fix it firmly in place with strong waterproof tape, covering any sharp ends. Make the net into a circle or diamond shape.

- Collect some water from the pond and pour it into a shallow white tray.

- Glide your net through the water. Put any creatures and plants that you catch in your net into the white tray to see them more clearly. <u>Always return any living things to the pond after a few minutes.</u>

PROTECTING LAKES AND PONDS

Look online to find ponds and lakes near your home. There might be a village pond, a duck pond near a playground, a boating lake or fishing lake, or a lake in a nature reserve. Ask an adult to take you to visit some ponds or lakes, and look out for ways you can help keep the ecosystem healthy.

Why are lakes and ponds important?

Over 97 per cent of our planet's water is the salt water in the oceans. Much of the fresh water is frozen in glaciers or at the poles. Only a tiny amount is found in lakes and ponds. It provides a home to many plants and animals that cannot live in salt water. Fresh water is essential for amphibians and many insects to live and breed in, and without them, the balance of nature would be drastically disrupted.

Pollution

Freshwater lakes are easily polluted. Fertilisers and pesticides are spread by the rain and wind and make their way into the water. Chemicals from factories and sewage waste from towns also wash into lakes via rivers and streams. They not only kill animals, but can lead to an increase in algae (see page 25), which in turn means that other species cannot survive.

Waste from human activities often ends up in rivers, lakes and ponds.

HOW CAN YOU HELP?

- Never throw rubbish into the water. Take it home and recycle it or put it in the bin.

- Don't pour chemicals down the sink or drain. Dispose of paint, medicine and oil at your local recycling centre.

- Use less water at home. Don't leave the tap running when you clean your teeth.

- Use eco-friendly cleaning products if you can.

- Take part in family clean-up days at lakes and rivers.

QUIZ

1. What name is given to a beaver's home?

a. Hollow

b. Lodge

c. Den

2. How do tadpoles breathe in the water?

a. With gills

b. With frills

c. With gales

3. What are a catfish's whiskers called?

a. Barbels

b. Bangles

c. Bundles

4. What colour are an egret's feathers?

a. Brown

b. Blue

c. White

5. How were North America's Great Lakes formed?

a. By a river

b. By glaciers

c. By a volcano

6. Which is the saltiest?

a. The Mediterranean Sea

b. The Dead Sea

c. The Caspian Sea

7. What enables creatures to walk on the water's surface?

a. Skater skin

b. Water repellence

c. Surface tension

8. What is the name for a rapid increase in algae growth?

a. Algal bloom

b. Algal flourish

c. Algal surge

ANSWERS: 1b. 2a. 3a. 4c. 5b. 6b. 7c. 8a.

GLOSSARY

algae (singular = **alga**) plant-like living things without roots

condense change from a gas to a liquid

consumer in a food chain, a creature that eats plants or other creatures

crater a bowl-shaped hollow made by a volcano

ecosystem a network of interacting living things

evaporate change from a liquid to a gas

glacial lake a lake formed by the movement of a glacier

hibernate going into a state of deep sleep to survive through the winter

larva the young form of an insect

metamorphosis the process of changing from a young form to an adult in two or more stages

moulting to get rid of an outer layer

nocturnal active at night

nutrient a substance that provides essential nourishment for living and growing

nymph the young form of an insect

organism a living thing, such as bacteria, plants, or animals

oxbow lake a lake formed from a U-shaped bend in a river

photosynthesis the way plants and algae produce food

precipitation moisture falling to the ground as rain, snow, sleet or hail

producer the first part of a food chain, consisting of plants and algae

pupa an insect in its young form between larva and adult

reservoir a lake used to store water for people to use

stagnant body of water which stands still and has no flow or current

tectonic lake a lake formed by movement in the Earth's crust

transpiration (for a plant) giving off water vapour

volcanic lake a lake formed in the crater of a volcano

INDEX

FURTHER READING

These websites and books will give you lots more ideas about the great outdoors!

www.wildlifetrusts.org/about-us

www.fsc-uk.org/en-uk

www.woodlandtrust.org.uk/naturedetectives

www.rspb.org.uk/fun-and-learning/for-kids
  facts-about-nature

www.nationaltrust.org.uk/children-and-nature

www.discoverwildlife.com

www.fws.gov/index.html

British Insects and other Minibeasts (Nature in Your Neighbourhood)
Clare Collinson (Franklin Watts, 2015)

Insects and Spiders (Visual Explorers)
Paul Calver and Toby Reynolds (Franklin Watts, 2019)

Pond Wildlife (The Great Nature Hunt)
Clare Hibbert (Franklin Watts, 2016)

The Water Cycle (Geographics)
Georgia Amson-Bradshaw (Franklin Watts, 2017)